for Mudge,
for her
Italian soul!

**THE COLDEST
YEAR OF GRACE**

SELECTED POEMS OF

GIOVANNI RABONI

TRANSLATED BY
STUART FRIEBERT
& VINIO ROSSI

THE COLDEST
YEAR OF GRACE

 **WESLEYAN UNIVERSITY PRESS**
Middletown, Connecticut

All inquiries and permission requests should be addressed to the Publisher, Wesleyan University Press, 110 Mt. Vernon Street, Middletown, Connecticut 06457.

Distributed by Harper & Row Publishers, Keystone Industrial Park, Scranton, Pennsylvania 18512.

Library of Congress Cataloging in Publication Data
Raboni, Giovanni, 1932–
The coldest year of grace.
I. Title.
PQ4878.A2C6 1984   851'.914   84-7363
ISBN 0-8195-5114-7 (alk. paper)
ISBN 0-8195-6116-9 (pbk.: alk. paper)

Manufactured in the United States of America

First Edition
Wesleyan Poetry in Translation

CONTENTS

III DECEPTIVE CADENCE

IV THE COLDEST YEAR OF GRACE

ACKNOWLEDGMENTS

We wish to thank Giovanni Raboni for taking such good care of us in Milan and going over all the translations of the poems, as well as Oberlin College for a grant that helped us immeasurably. We also thank David Young, for extremely useful suggestions all along.

Some of these translations have appeared in the following journals under the following titles: *Alchemy*: "Conversation about Nothing"; *Central Park*: "Birthday"; *Cutbank*: "Keys for an Unwritten Poem," "Woman's Song"; *Denver Quarterly*: "From the Altar in the Shadow"; *Field*: "The Dead and the True," "Pontius P.," "Bad Year," "Christmas Morning," "The Colonial Error," "Afternoon Movies," "This Is the Catalogue," "Little Comedy," "Magdalen's Fear," "Hospital Interns"; *Helix*: "Peter's Betrayal," "Expert Opinion," "Figures in the Park," "Squaring Off," "The Commemoration," "The Remorse of St. John the Baptist"; *Little Balkans Review*: "Serenade"; *Malahat Review*: "Aria for Tenor," "The Checkroom," "Meditation in the Orchard," "Simulated & Dissimulated," "Judas' Oration," "Elements of an Urban Landscape"; *Poet Lore*: "Office Secrets," "Career of the Brute," "Otherwise"; *Poetry Now*: "Mirror," "The Cooked and the Raw," "Expert Opinion"; *Quarterly West*: "Tablecloth," "Summer in the Villa Brianza," "Notice," "Rain," "Doorway," "Suicide in the Infirmary," "Dawn," "Novel," "The Unwholesomeness of the Air"; *West Branch*: "More Interviews"; *Willow Springs Magazine*: "Moving," "Madrigal," "Moon."

"The Feet That We Don't Have," "Another Life," "From the Numbers," "Once, on the Steps," "It Happened Once," and "We Have Friends" appeared originally in *New Directions Anthology No. 43* (New York: New Directions, 1981). "The Coldest Year of Grace" appeared originally in *45 Contemporary Poems*, edited by Alberta Turner (New York: Longman, 1985).

INTRODUCTION

Giovanni Raboni was born in Milan, Italy, in 1932. He still makes his home there and works as an editor for Mondadori Publishers. His first major collection, *L'Insalubrità dell'Aria* (*The Unwholesomeness of the Air*), appeared in 1963, and its poems are anchored in place and history. The poems seem at times spoken by a prosecuting attorney building a case against waste and corruption in secular and religious circles. The poet-guide walking us through the ruins is a sort of modern-day Virgil, with an eye for searing details and an admonishing tone that threatens to put us all on trial.

Le Case della Vetra (*The Houses of the Vetra*) followed in 1966, with poems that assume, as the dominant landscape, a defunct square in Milan bordered today by the church of San Lorenzo and a porno movie house. The Vetra was originally a popular quarter, crossed by a canal that emptied into a larger basin, the Naviglio. Weaving through the poems, this waterway reminds us of Lethe, but no one gets to the other side, and anyone resembling a boatman turns out to be more interested in saving himself. In earlier times, a tower marked the site of public hangings, and the Vetra particularly evokes the plague of 1630–31, when anointers accused of spreading contagion were executed there. Raboni moves back and forth between historical events, long since forgotten, and current horrors, and there are savage reminders that nothing much has changed: ". . . if someone / devours a baby girl, or wrings the neck / of an old laundress (she was starching / Mussolini's collars, by the way), there's no remedy; / not for him, not for them, there's no Christ."

Cadenza d'Inganno (*Deceptive Cadence*) appeared in 1975. True to the musical principle to which the title alludes, the pieces in this volume take on a mysterious, half-finished cast and seem to end in midair, so the reader is forced to complete them. The "I" of the settings is caught up in what appear to be tiny troubles, and seems to be sleepwalking; and the landscapes are much more intensely personal than in Raboni's previous work. Once again, though, no single experience or vision is clarified, and objects loom up suddenly: ". . . first the headboard, / then the springs, the sides— / my mother's bed." The reader is often left frozen in some dream that is on its way to becoming nightmare.

In 1978, *Il Piu' Freddo Anno di Grazia* (*The Coldest Year of Grace*) was published. In one line it catches the mood of all Raboni's books, from the earliest, historically oriented, poems—in which emotions play off historical, political, and autobiographical aspects of Italy, the way light plays off objects in impressionistic paintings—to the almost filmic, journalistic "interviews" of the middle years, and on to the latest voice prints, love poems of a special kind.

This selection proceeds chronologically, representing the major poems in each book, with the exception of the most recent collection, *Nel Grave Sogno* (*In the Deep Dream*), 1982. A handful of poems from this book show Raboni turning from affinities with near-contemporaries, Sbarbaro, Rebora, and Campana, toward understatement and elusiveness, and we wanted to feature this tender and modest side of his latest work because we feel it is Raboni at his most evocative. The poems that close our selection are reminiscent of Montale, the great classic poet of twentieth-century Italian literature. Indeed, one has only to set Raboni's poem "Notice" next to Montale's "In limine" to sense their vibrant relationship. However, it is also clear that Raboni strikes out on his own, especially in the haunting "Hospital Interns," which confronts, with biblical force, the death of a complicated friend before the altar of modern medicine.

Influence and affection aside, Raboni has also translated from many languages. His Baudelaire is a striking achievement, and he is currently translating Proust. In addition, he has written extensively on contemporary poetry and poetics, showing an emerging interest in English-language poetry; his essays on Auden, Pound, and Eliot are highly regarded. A glance at his bibliography reveals a wide-ranging, altruistic interest in many other writers and literatures as well.

Raboni's study in Milan is filled with paintings, sculpture, huge stacks of magazines and, on a narrow desk, piles of new books. (He is known for his interest in young writers, and will frequently call one with words of encouragement.) The desk looks out on a small park, with trees; a place to read and think. It resembles Raboni's poetic world, the window like one in seventeenth-century painting, illuminating a private, interior space. This world befits Raboni's poetry, which is soft-spoken on the surface but fairly bristling with implications, ideas, and passions. The poems seem to enter his work-life through a definite space, like the window over his desk, but nothing comes too loudly or looms too large. The poet inhabits this world discreetly, measuring it with a deeply ingrained reticence: "Speak from a distance or just be quiet," from La Fontaine's *Fables*, was taken by Raboni as an epigraph for one of his collections.

In poem after poem, paradoxically, the dominant element is the sharpness of this silence, underlined by strong details. The voice, the narrative itself, is left fragmented, and ghostly shapes and tones emerge that can become solid enough to stumble against. The method amounts to a moral analogue of Raboni's aesthetics: the strategy is watching others, "to learn / which story is theirs, who hunts them." Half turned away from his subjects and objects, at times even muttering to himself, the poet shows us in poignant glimpses not only what is essential in the human condition, but also what must be ignored: ". . . I can't change / it, from afar it fulfills me, freezes me." In other words, there is just an instant when one might escape, if one could only reject a sense of fulfillment that sets in like seduction.

Raboni's way with understatement is to *see into*, or *put into*, or *take out of* both things and people a multiplicity of meanings. By bits and snatches the poems build to their cumulative effects, defining person and place at the last moment of their existence. He is aware that as we approach the moment of nonexistence, everything grows more complex, more evil, and the only way out, in his view, is a sort of almost mindless repetition that might just spark renewal: "Perhaps everything really has to be done again and again / injustice is in the air." His fresh answer to this dilemma is to use the twin modes of poeticization and politicization to drive the poem home. Poeticizing is the deepening of an image, or the particular moment in reality, to echo concomitant images, whereas politicizing, the politicizing of specific issues—injustice, calumny, out-and-out evil—leads us to examine the social implications of these images or ideas. One must not be allowed to obfuscate the other. At the crucial moment, the poem must break off poeticizing and state things we finally wonder about, because we are, after all, beings in search of morals: "But down deep what if it's right / that way?"

What has brought us to this state, prepared our way, is both dead *and* true. And sympathetic vibrations result, of the musical sort, which may shatter our false or willful vision, permitting us to see anew. Political statement parallels poetic image, reinforces it, doubling its chances of lasting in our consciousness; but the two are not permitted to mix, and hence retain a purity that enables us to see clearly by each. And the metaphor has been frozen at its climactic moment, before any (false) synthesis might be reached.

Like any good poet, Raboni is preoccupied with the sound of poetry, and there are signs of the emphasis he places on music everywhere, from the mixing of semantic and sonorous sense in words themselves to the very title of one collection, *Cadenza d'Inganno*. It is in the more subtle situation of the "I" who speaks, or sings, these poems in a sort of recitative that Raboni can be said to be a modern master. This "I," partly the voice in the poet's head, partly the reader's to possess, seemingly abstruse about its place in the poems, slides up and down the rhythms of memory, from the bluntest exchanges between misbegotten lovers to the spiritual inner speech we seek refuge in from other selves, from our other selves: ". . . the things said and not said / between you, and the person you are / are probably too few or too many, I wonder / what it's like to travel on after you . . ." Here the father's voice mingles with his daughter's as he looks for her, looks after her, in his worry, the voice moving obliquely among its many cares; from a clinical, almost repressed balance to casual, heartbroken plaintiveness so suddenly as to take our breath away and shock us with his sense of loss, his lost bearing. Finally, the "I" of these poems is never completely objective, but lets us see and feel clearly what is seen and felt, and that may be quite enough: "I have my stories . . . / But if in the middle of the mirror with its gilded frame, in / the middle, the darkness of the mirror, you are there . . ."

Now at the height of his considerable powers, Raboni is likely to continue to work in ways that will interest serious readers of contemporary poetry. His international breadth and eclectic concerns, his knowledge of history and our place in it, combined with his deft mix of regional and worldly language, satisfy a major demand made of artists: that they heighten the specific in the universal.

I

THE UNWHOLESOMENESS OF THE AIR

Notice

Just a few words,
just a notice on the backside of the bill
miscalculated by the owner.
Perhaps it's too late, perhaps the wheel
turns too much for something to remain:
eyes quartered, horse heads,
nice days of Guernica.
Splinters turn to pulp here.
And even I who write to you
from this unchanged place
I have no sentences for you, I have no
voice for this faith I still have,
for the symmetrical flasks, the rectangular
crude chairs of straw.
I no longer have any sight or certainty; it's as though
all of a sudden the pen
had slipped from my hand
and I were writing with my elbow or my nose.

The Deeds of the Devil in the City of ★★★

Living here perhaps
one becomes, as you say,
more opaque, freer each day;
the mist lets up more and more,
grows thinner each winter. Well, I know them
too, you see, these tricks of the devil,
between the debtbook and twine, double keys
and elevators—your devil-banker,
specialist in lids: and if you
have business with him, with *protocol*, live in peace
with everyone, you age well. Surely it's then,
it's thus that you pay. Even if something's
still outside, the memorial
of the hanged man, love's grimaces
on urinal walls . . .

Restoration

Of all this
there's no longer anything left (or perhaps something
can be guessed at, there's still some road
cobbled in part for the carts, and an inn . . .).
My father used to say that people
around here, from Piazza della Vetra behind
San Lorenzo, were
likely to leave the house with a knife
at seven in the evening. Of course, the Naviglio
is just two steps away; the fog used to be thicker
before they covered it, the square
filled with stalls, with acetylene
lamps, roasted chestnuts
in black pans, swallowers
of nails, scoops, serving spoons, even
pieces of dishes, surely not a place
to stroll by with your girl. But just like that,
they've demolished houses, destroyed neighborhoods,
here and elsewhere (the Vetra, Fiori Chiari, the Bottonuto);
what good does that do? The harm was not
in those steps, certain doors
with their peepholes, courtyards suffocated
by long, run-down balconies you went along
to your door: the steps are rickety, there's
a dampness that'll catch you your death.
If my father were alive, I'd even ask him:
do you think it's any good? and the way
they're doing it? It seems to me
the harm's never in things, I'd tell him.

Conversation about Nothing

It should have been another idea: talk about it
a few more evenings, fake
having made a decision, decline in the end.
There were pros and cons, you see. (Everyone
agreed about that.) By the end of January
we reached this point, having
faith in time, a little like the auctioneer waiting
for the third candle to be consumed.

The Unwholesomeness of the Air

From this green relic,
from the bits of grass, what
do the tourists expect? It's true, it rains
a lot here too; the clouds make shade;
hedges, stone balls hide the damp gardens,
villas that smell musty enough
to drive the tenants out (and in October
they're hard to heat) or the turreted embattlements
where it's even possible the specter
of a proto-industrialist moves about. But here,
the map of the countryside is pierced by brambles
of those famous Lombards;
the pride of the shark, the ambition
of the worker,
           the tenacious obsession with
success that transforms the artisan
into a small-time contractor, the shops
into trusts and monopolies,
                the good humor
of the stockholders. Here the rabbit won't run;
not even if you pay him; if you
mutter "the Duchess," he keeps quiet,
so quiet in his cage made
of packing crates.

Afternoon Movies

Nearly always at this hour
people arrive who are somewhat special (making
a good impression). Some sit down
but then keep changing their seats;
some remain standing at the back of the hall, sniffing,
sniffing out the rare passages, the little girl,
half-imbecile, the lady who enters alone,
the lame girl . . . Well, what
can one do? I watch them to learn
which story is theirs, who hunts them. When
the lights come on, one thinks how
the heart must wring looking for
safety a little farther off, sinking
into the darkness, which will return in a minute.

Jobs on the Underground Railroad
During the Month of November

They'd say they were few in number, as always: one
seated way up in the crane, careful to see
that it rises and falls;
another two or three with drills,
pneumatic hammers, etc.; someone
mixes the mortar with his hoe;
about ten in all. And this hole
fringed by the shadows of the huge
Giolittian buildings (black and silent
witnesses to gold money)
on the Cordusio, in the via Dante, doesn't it seem
almost a private matter?
As though they just worked for themselves, for those friends
of their invisible race—not for the ones
wandering along the brink, brushing up against the lanterns,
drawing out autumn's sins . . .

Office Secrets

But to
study the furnishings in detail
you ought to know several things, friend: the curve
of the bench, for example, the thickness of the leather,
the size of the nails or the spines,
the capacity (in cubic millimeters/per day) of the little tubes
dispensing the serum
etc. etc.

And tell them for me, friend, we're among the dead.

Christmas Morning

The scullions of the prince, friend of my friends,
come out early into the square
that's covered with snow
in their white aprons, their teeth chattering from the cold,
call out and wave casseroles
to the people passing by, who are so thin
they almost disappear: a chestnut
vendor, a soldier, someone playing
bagpipes, two chimney sweeps . . .
get them to file quickly through the huge wet gate
of the palace, then down to the suffocating
kitchens—help serve in the little chapel—
and this is unspeakably profane—
a roast duck on a pavement of ice.

Doorway

Difficult to say
how many swords, how many lances, how many leather helmets
on Roman profiles,
how many smiths and fishermen with conical hoods
and pointed ears,
how many pig or dragon faces, how many feet
with five toes

and wheels and crooked cakes and projections
of well-stocked tables

in the crowd, in the fire, in the joy
of snow that comes close, of wine
drunk when we were young,
of the bristling, lively crowd, of a whole country
that fishes, hunts, etc. and prepares
the acrid feast upon the wood.

Surely, it's time to speak out
as it was once time to remain silent
with everyone (even friends), careful
not to go the same route, ever;
never to leave torn
notebooks about, witch-hunting addresses . . . And time helps,
well, isn't it true? (Too much, even.) Time helps
to find yourself again, close the soul's wounds.
Wounds, resuscitating the Etc. But if you
are barely astute, you know it's not necessary
to let youself go. And so, no hugs
for the Negro baritone, the Jewish
scientist from his mother, the citizen
malgré lui from overseas
torn to pieces by More and Less: no flowers
on the graves or uncivil reproaches
to the warders. The more you expect it,
the more the breeze blows for the hoods
of all the executioners.

The Colonial Error

I know: but who has the courage
to take them for pigs? If I think of them
one by one: the first, a poor slob
of a gardener or cook, come
from God knows where
to tell a story of witches—
perhaps dreamt, perhaps invented, certainly
not true; the second, to write on sheets,
practically scraps, with twisted letters,
a true denunciation; someone
to whom nothing matters, who just
wants to go off to sleep
till tomorrow; the third, a policeman
with cigar and bowler,
ready to box the ears of any suspect
or bring him a drink of water
in a paper cup; all of them, even
the colonial judge, an upright man,
corrupt,
with his abstract wig of pastry tubes,
all of them, even the guards in high stockings,
khaki jackets, caps with visors,
tying him to that stake in the desert—
there we go—looking at them one by one,
who has the courage to jump them? And then again,
as Gide says through that little boy talking of Christ,
il fallait bien qu'on le cloue pour qu'il tienne.

Pontius P.

15

In the depths
of a horrible country that has no winter, rector
of hotheads, judge of disputes
without rhyme or reason
—what else can the most malign of the
fathers want? Only in dreams he brings me back
to the engraved green of meadows, the pleasures of a time
that does not return: putting a horse through the trot
all alone,
the delicate rustic exploits,
the dress coats that strangle the fox
beyond the last hedge.
      Reality
is the squalor of voyages, the ill-digested career,
recommendations that serve no purpose
or arrive too late; it's having, instead
of the gray, early-morning stagnant pool, filled
with indolent game,
this dirty basin I wash my hands in.

More Interviews

The Carpenter

If you seek
you find. If you want to save some wood,
instead of nailing it into a square
or an isosceles triangle or a circle,
you can make it into a cross.

The Washerwoman

I looked for the blood
in this livid face, curdled
on linen.
I struck the plait of wash
on the usual stone
to blot out the pus spots.
I gathered up the chest. I set out
on my way, struggling.

The Surgeon

There are blows, and blows. There are grazing wounds
no one can heal
and men who die at eighty
of knife wounds suffered in youth.
There's no rule. Someone saves himself
and becomes a priest. Someone's sight
weakens. At times
knives point up from the heart
in the direction of the blade.

The Fortune Teller

The day will come when
it's the doctors' turn
with their glasses on their noses.
One day bishops will have
brooms like war-horses
or at least they'll talk about them.
There'll come a day when
for having seen him die
over and over again
They'll no longer notice.

The Baker

I'll not ask for
advice here and there.
I know what I have to do.
No leaven, a certain amount of flour.
Each morning I'll get up at dawn,
as always, as now.
It's just a question of thickness.
Living, I'll be
the sword of the dead
staring at the water, the ashes,
the arrogance of the apprentices.

Rain

What rain,
what an ugly night for the dead, you said.
Even I think of certain dead at times, when the sky
clouds over: the girl dead of Spanish flu
in '17 (flowers on the tomb
even this year); of Crespi,
killed by brigands, they say: he was returning
from Milan to Saronno: but maybe he killed himself
with his carbine; of the father
of great-grandmother Mariani, prefect
under Maria Theresa, who was the guest
listed in her land register,
soaking and rotting away . . .

Keys for an Unwritten Poem

You have to know certain things
to understand history. The city
you see at the beginning is not Bergamo,
it's Cremona (see also the allusion
to 1751, year of the transfer). Then: the old
woman, robust but a bit weak in the head
who threatens her daughter with a can—taunts her;
widowed at forty
she married an apprentice at the mill: which explains,
among other things, that business of surnames. *The assistant
    opposite*
is the man who supervises the masons
on behalf of the customer in contrast
to the flunky of the contractor. The war
that was about to break out
was the war of '15–'18.

Bad Year

It was the night the vase
slowly went to pieces, shifting
the way grain slides in the cupboard
between the rat's paws. That night
grandpa went out into the garden as always
to finish his Virginia. In Bergamo
it's cold in the trees now. He thought
about drought and hail, lost harvests,
about the end of the world: a sure thing now
after so many disasters and uncertainties
of the seasons. Perhaps he thought about
what happened later: the farmers,
frightened by the crisis and needing
money, crowded around the tellers' windows
to close their accounts. A bank
for small businesses
—commercial or agricultural—
won't put up a fight if all at once
savings dry up. That happened
afterward. That night, in that darkness,
the vase ended up as dust, simply consumed itself
along its slender crack, as through
a confused clepsydra.

Summer in the Villa at Brianza

Summer in the villa at Brianza
with grandma sick and portraits of grandpa
dead in twenty-nine,
suppose it's of this I speak to you.
She keeps to herself, full of scruples,
upstairs, at the end of a wing of the house, inside
a telescope of dusty rooms;
he in flight forever, from the study
kept half in mourning, from the room
of dry wines and billiards . . .
They were too many, these two invisible people:
or too little light filtered in
through the Persian blinds. And instead, what emotion
at the dinner hour! The fire lit as a joke,
the tablecloth spotted with sauce,
the exquisite cheese from the factory
in the sharp odor the night made. Then,
the anguish, someone going upstairs,
someone false-stepping, stumbling in the pitiful corridor,
between the abandoned rooms.
They were too many, these two invisible people:
too many for the boy who spun out
prayers
in the dark; he thought he was standing vigil,
struggling with the furniture in walnut.

The Dead and the True

In the damp house, the little
that is dry seems even drier:
in the bedroom on the first floor
the wooden floorboards, almost white,
unwaxed and a bit
distant, below in the billiard
room, the ivory skittles
set in a cross . . . (Sooner or later I return
to see the house of friends
where a son is about to be born
—it happened two days later—and we waited
in the evening for the storm to bring
a little fresh air down to Milan. Pallid,
all along the walls, their faces like pimps
or hypocrites
Lombardian forefathers
went over the count of the eggs
and cheese: using their shrewdness and huge quantities
of goose quills. You would laugh at them,
disgusted. But down deep what if it's right
that way? Better than our real ones, people,
distracted, melancholy
because of more subtle flaws; capable of behaving like
bourgeoise even in death—or scouring
Africa, like grandpa; who knows
that will not be the sort of forefathers
our son will feign having, laughing
at them, turning his back on them
the way no one has ever been able to.)

II

THE HOUSES OF THE VETRA

Tablecloth

What's the use of talking to friends?
Nearly all of them get angry, or laughing
slap their forehead. You talk of money troubles,
of singers growing old or thin. Outside
night puffs up like an owl.
And we're just a few, too few to suffer
so many counts of indictment:
the egg, the bread, the glass
set on the table
like so many sober instruments of torture.

Novel

What the hell are we going to talk about
in the house of the hanged man
if we can't ever talk about rope?
These were—
that night, in far-off
nineteen hundred and sixty et cetera
as he climbed
three small marble steps leading up
to the elevator—
more or less
the thoughts of a certain young man
about whom, for the moment,
I don't have the time, the will, the desire
to think any longer.

Woman's Song

When it rains they're just disgusting—
those windows covered with grease, the stove
sending smoke into the corners and in the kitchen
the salt stopped up, the oilcloth
sticking . . . but feeling good
or feeling bad, that's something else again.
The children going up and down
the little balcony outside, snapping dry branches
with the sides of their bodies, frightened, somewhat gnomelike
judging by their eyes: they seem about to fly
over the roof. But I say that from here,
to want to return to where I was, thin
from hunger, worn out by lice,
there's a great difference.

The Career of the Brute

In a flash
you call a poor fellow *brute* (even if
he's really a poor devil): but just think
what a tangle, what darkness,
how many difficult things to name
for a mug like him and a day
like this one!
        In the end, you see,
it's the gesture that decides: if someone
devours a baby girl, or wrings the neck
of an old laundress (she was starching
Mussolini's collars, by the way), there's no remedy;
not for him, not for them, there's no Christ.

Otherwise

Just try to think
that one does not want to take away from anyone
the strength not to believe:
and that for this very reason miracles occur
only to those other people, and only
in the most stifled, invisible chinks,
in the plaster footprint you can't inspect:
the news that arrives not a second later,
the dreamt impulse that makes you cross
the street at the moment—
someone who dies solely for having pulled you out of a jam;
otherwise you wouldn't know what to do.

City from Above

These streets that go up to the walls
have no horizon, see: they bump into a white,
clean sky, without trees, like a river that bends. From here to the
    processions
where the gentlemen and their dogs walk along,
you can't tell who's holding the leash and their tails
are up like little flags.
There must be ninety steps, a hundred, but no more:
farther down in the heart of the city
divided into quarters (you can count them) and delicate, soft-lined
as a washbasin . . . and a bit farther on
the cathedral, with its five superimposed orders: continue
on the right, on a diagonal for another
thirty or forty steps—measuring away: you're still looking at it
as if on a map—you hit the axis of the square
built on the rocky foundation of the Roman
circus

silent gray ellipse where
enormous, obese, fattened people sleep
or drag around like capons, crammed full
of meat and Burgundy so they won't escape from the square! The
    poor
of the city. Halfway between the foci
there, in four hundred years,
the guillotine will be installed.

The Baked and the Raw

Dig them up after ten years. At Musocco
they need room and room is made
by stacking the dead one on top of the other, sealed
in a piece of wall. Move one section after another. This month
it's Section 49, where my father is buried. You really wouldn't want
to leave him in that hole
of nightmares: body with bricks: after a while
you'll never feel like coming
to visit him. Enough of that; I never even
used to go, it's the truth, I wouldn't even
go to the country cemetery
he'd seen when he was still alive and I think
he would have loved it. But now, maybe now
that he no longer wants these things, they're even
less important now: the fragrance
of the grass, the poverty of the cross,
the name cleared by the rain. Maybe he understands
a piece of wall better, feels
the just angles, works of mortar, mixing
sand and lime, connecting the baked
and the raw, the corners, the bones of his neighbors . . .

Elements of an Urban Landscape

32

Not right here, the bocce court was nearby. If you'd arrived
five minutes sooner
there were things you remember,
the blue marking chalk (someone
squashed a leaf),
the wrought-iron tray on the bank.

The normal procedure

obtained: appeals, scuffling,
and dust fills your eyes and amen.

The Checkroom

One thing, if nothing else, you have to grant him:
he could no longer leave things in such
order. If you look around
from the dog cage to the Colt's
holster, from the box of samples to the calculator
there's not an atom out of place; with the files
shut till tomorrow you can climb up
on the plastic chair and from there, before
the sirens sound,
look into the depths of the well.

Expert Opinion

34

Not so far away
or so close, at a middle
distance, say, confident, sure that everything will end again
with them blackmailing each other,
perhaps later in an embrace. But examination
of the point of entry and the point of exit
does not confirm said trajectory
or distance, the lovers drawn in chalk
do not confirm it: here we have a man, a woman against
the folding seats—in all senses of the word
without a scratch, moving off slowly in the sinless flotsam
from one mile to the next along the service road.

Figures in the Park

And just think there are
spacious curves along these lanes, low
hedges you can see through . . .
                       With my poor eyesight I wonder
how I manage to see them at all. Who knows. They come up from
   below,
come down from above,
from behind the markers of the rare plants,
moving cautiously, silently, their ties carefully knotted,
their horns filled with moss, their tails low;
they don't ask or tell the time
to the people we see passing by.
They file along, hunting at the edge of the pond.

Poor witch, poor wretch, he'd repeat, smoothing his mustache,
his hair, carefully adjusting his tie,
laughing in his heart because she'll fall in the pond.

On the bench he folds his underwear
and bandages carefully, adjusts his crutch,
opens and closes the paper sacks of gravel and suppositories,
ready to be redeemed or slaughtered.

3 and 1/2 feet tall but
capable of rolling a cask with a branch
along slight inclines, unraveling
garbage, the wicker baskets full of trash, crosses. She's a cube
of dust moving toward
the low-lying trap of the pond.

A slight
indication, like the quantity
of dust on a shoe alone or the manner
of wiping sweat from the forehead;
I seized it: the hunted monster, the assassin,
the man who kills under a full moon
and I run shooting sparks from my skates on the asphalt to fetch
the slow, buzzing, steel mopeds of the police.

The Commemoration of the Defunct

With you and yours, we realize
you've found a modus vivendi. It wasn't easy
or hard; there was almost no choice. But those fellows
who never take you in, charred
in the carcass of the fighter plane, nibbled by the lion, cut down
by typhus on the plateau—what
salvation in them is there for you? What sin
in your squinting eyes for them, the way you keep looking
at the newspaper. Wouldn't it be
better to let it drop—here I am as I am though
rarely
trotting briskly, conscience-stricken, along the main
road to the cemetery
on All Soul's Day. We were displaced persons—
one night yes one night not going to visit
relatives, neighbors, you could read the names
of the gates in the circle of the flashlight,
as today on the tombs: or
not later than yesterday in the vault
plated with armor, truly a submarine, the gloomy
unfastening of the strange boxes . . .
Let them be returned, I say (the dead) to our daily hash, fold your
   paper,
let the living bury the living, from afar.

This Is the Catalogue

And then, if you go around on foot you'll end up
knowing them all: the big old ladies
of the via Lazzaretto, animated
and in groups like cronies, gossiping: the modest
middle-class women, almost lugubrious, waiting
between the Ponte Vetero and the Arena:
the blonde from Cinque vie
with her swollen face. So you see
it's utterly different from the big boulevards
where the girls are healthy and slender
and stroll along laughing among
the people with their hoods turned up
to the clear, bright light of the armored cars . . .

Birthday

In the empty city, full of sun, projection
of the dawn. The edge of light
bends, drops down. You see
half of it adrift in the shadows. From the eaves
there comes a very sharp whistle, light as
if in another quarter, beyond the complex
circle of the Vigorelli race track; in the roar
of air conditioning
your son was being born again.

Dispute

A woman abruptly
got up out of bed saying,
"You can't do that." And frets about, pulling
stuff from drawers, hung up in the space
between chest and clothes tree, nearly
tipping the lamp over, the basin—and
haughty in her shoes
brushes up against the mirror-fog, touches
her head every now and then with the palm of her hand,
sprays the fixative-insecticide on her hair.

To My Son in the Country

When the lights go out in the country
so many people pop up who'd disappeared
pieces of dominoes coagulate on the ground
branches enter from the window's darkness
and say, Well, well . . . (you have to be
patient with the Illuminating Co.) and you feel the blows
losing their color, the livid spots waiting for
the snail, the mamma, the caterpillar,
the talking cricket with the candle.

Enough Room

42

Time passes, we feel
more grandiose each day: we're still,
however, the people who raise an eyebrow
or scratch the tip of their nose, go on
thinking that sorts like that (he who
glides along with no eyelids, he who
makes love with forks and cord) are,
compared to us, someone else—and don't understand
there's enough room for each one of them
in each one of us.

Little Comedy

Not that it means much to me, you know. It's not at all
obligatory. And I always have these things
on me, the twig for peeling, the half-wit's
profile for carving on the walking stick.
Let's not talk about it anymore, don't you agree? (The train
starts up again. It's never darker than it is now.)

Album of War Memories

One room
is a box whose floor slopes 15 or 20°
where the cat is bigger than the zebra
and each corner's a bridgehead, the arrival platform of a conveyor
    belt that keeps feeding
ignition keys and tires, munition cases, number and penetrability
    of the soldiers' bodies.

Another room
is a sort of attic or furnace
not yet finished
and with fire overhead; it'd be enough to keep me happy, sitting
on the straw of four demijohns.

The third room
is hollowed out of the interior of a sphere;
I'd say divide it so there's room
for a bed, a chair, a table and a machine gun
and in the other half (lengthwise) an infirmary
for more complicated treatments.

Simulated & Dissimulated

For my son

45

We wanted to get—
I with my mole's vision, you simulating
a slight and gloomy limp—up to the esplanade
where the band is playing. Yes, I knew
"only military marches":
but this whole staging, all of a sudden . . . Even the spot
seems somewhere else, an abandoned bocce court,
an old cement tennis court. At the back,
fifteen policemen in a row, in shirt sleeves,
firing into a wooden molding.

Suicide in the Infirmary

In a crowd of solid objects, drops of water
shining through. Peelings
of an orange. The sides of the bunk. And
the effort it took. Losing consciousness, as in sleep,
between two pillows, free of all anxiety, between a death
that drags and one that waits, just like that—
both timid, out of focus in the semicircle
of shade—you rouse yourself
all over again; just think of it, you grope for
the lamp's white spot, pinch your glasses on
to chase another death, closer to you,
like glass, plastic cardboard . . .

The Remorse of St. John the Baptist

Silence. Listen! I announce his death
because in your eyes I'm the author
of his coming and his disastrous
days. Oh, if I had only died first,
in the desert, the way camels die
who rely on their own gullet! I rely on
my own memory, the memory
that God concedes me of future things.
I didn't want to kill him,
but my faith was turned into stone or knife, my baptism
into a violent scorpion. May He forgive me
if I've sinned too little! I flourish on guilt
as the Virgin flourished on Him
in her involuntary womb.

Fear of the Magdalen

48

I'm afraid of wood and rock,
I'm afraid of the body, of the nerves that are lacerated,
of cut tendons, I'm afraid of light,
I'm afraid of the stone that will shut your door,
I'm afraid of the wind and of the voices, I'm afraid
of the crow that will eat you, I'm afraid of the wolf
that will find your bones, I'm afraid
that you're dead and every night
I'll be afraid you'll kiss me with ice
and pull my feet beneath the sheet.

Meditation in the Orchard

Remember: turn the gas off, turn the key six times.
There's the risk of splitting the chalice and the risk of losing it
before all is done.
And the orchard not yet filled, the ears still sound,
how many lost threads to knot
so that all be done!
To choose the right nails, choose bile and sponge,
rehearse with Anna and with Pilate,
discuss the wound with the knife throwers
so that everything be done.

Judas' Oration

O Israelites, black and white, companions
of my life in this fire and wind,

here, I extend you the hand of pardon:
I, sacrificer of the lamb and sacrificed

twice, in love and in hate
once apostle of the brotherly

olive, another of the suicidal
olive. And to you Romans, I extend the hand

of pardon, so that everything be done
twice, and each of us see with four eyes.

Peter's Betrayal

How many times, pilgrims—
beaten down by a stormy night,
settling down finally by the fire
at an inn, we find ourselves among
the tired faces of our enemies!
Certainly we should
rise up howling: maybe even
pull out a knife: and asked
our name
we could answer with more scorching words,
smashing crocks. But who would benefit
from so much bother? Not the barkeeper, not the heart
donc in by rain. Better to pretend we're friends
from abroad, or perhaps too vile: stretched out on the bench
that slides more and more into shadow in the sparks from the fire—
to answer with gestures, a simple yes or no,
and pull our cloaks up over our eyes.

Aria for Tenor

Crucify him
since that's the mandate
and tired old age draws near.
Nail him to the moves of the knight,
the viola player, the friend
who's too quick at dice.
And each time, at the palace or the grounds
of the marketplace,
forget your dreams and stab harder,
quick, to the hilt. Crucify him.

Dawn

It's daylight by now; it's not enough
to sit so gravely in your wicker chair
dressed in cane and blood
listening to the soldiers' insults, your side hosting
the lance's synthetic trace. To be day, you need
to have your eyes far from your cheek,
your nail spread out from the finger, sprinkling
a little bit of lime on your heart.

III

DECEPTIVE CADENCE

As Though Blind, with Anxiety

As though blind, with anxiety, against
the storm and the hail, one
after another, I closed
seven windows.
It was important I didn't know which ones.
Right at dawn, trembling,
with the horrible attention to details of those who lie awake or
    dying,
I understand that I've crept
into my customary darkness,
San Gregorio Street first floor,
on this side of my children,
of being able to hear or say a word.

Moving

Early in the morning
a step from the gate, I don't remember
whether in the street or the garden.
It wasn't closed or open. It could have
been very late. There might have been some wind.
It was necessary to run after them—to scream
sliding on the gravel,
shoving off from the stakes of the dahlias,
falling on the plane trees, flying
up the three steps of grit,
quickly, more quickly! before someone
(Gondrand, even then?) cursing
because there's too much walnut,
gasping blindly on the steps,
carried in—first the headboard,
then the springs, the sides—
my mother's bed.

Squaring Off

If this is what we're talking about and if
they continue to live like this—in the bite
of the oxide on the sheet-metal, or like mold
lapping up against the bottles—
you're right: we're wasting our money. But as for the dead,
there's other news coming down the wire later:
as though they remained close
to their bodies, uncertain, distrustful
of a provisional kind of corruption,
waiting for signs . . . And then you'd see
that our accounts would return, farther down the line, later.

Creditors

We try to speak
in two minutes, while someone adjusts
the curtains at the windows and friends
are already on the steps. Always there's
too little time when we have to settle
accounts with the dead. And so I tell
my mother to be patient—she,
who's close to dying, still
wants to know how my supper was . . .

Mirror

You have your stories: about rivals and inlaws who were barons
in Palermo and baldachin beds
where once when you were
a girl you woke up burned.
I have my stories: of great-grandfathers and great-uncles in high
    collars
involved with Austria and proper
docks on the lake—and thus
detest a piece of furniture that isn't dark or walnut.
But if in the middle of the mirror with its gilded frame, in
the middle, the darkness of the mirror, you are there . . .

Supine

62

If you lie on your back
the weight of your breasts,
calming themselves, becomes tenderness, just tenderness.
   Suddenly
there's no need to hide it: you can no longer play because it's
   tender and spent
and innocent and enough of that now.

False and Tendentious News

Cold in Europe, darkness over Italy.
Power is repugnant, like the hands of a barber.
                    —Osip Mandelstam

1

Even this evening, after supper, we talked about the quality of the
    soil.
Was it really soil from Morgiate?
If so, we'd done very badly to sign.
Someone, saying soil, was confused.

(In dream: evidence: the boots:
rubber perhaps, perhaps black,
with rust spots and blood like an old pocket knife.)

(And around one, when
the angel of kerosene bangs the mica shutters,
it began raining in the darkness
harder and harder, farther off,
separating soles from topsoil,
loosening topsoil into clods, clods to mud.)

2

Staying in the country I live my death.
Hanging from the trestles, flower beds,
from the roots of the wisteria, the rays of the wheel,
I'm waiting (the jar of Nescafé
within reach, the flint
between the fingers of my toes)
for the archangel Calabresi to descend and judge me.

3

The topic, unfortunately, came up at five o'clock.
We didn't know much; the telephone was out of order,
the carrier pigeons closely watched.
Someone, returning from the country, told
about having caught a glimpse of stable boys, dwarves, hands.
It was then (there are still some who regret it,
who embroider crests of chains unconsciously)
that together, trembling, we began to doubt
seditiously the word of the constable.

4

One thing, and this is it: the lesson's well taken.
If our levity is written on the trees
we'll erase it with our teeth,
we'll swallow names and bark.
To no one does it any longer occur to start screaming
it wasn't the communists who set the Reichstag on fire.

Afterward

1

Drawn in chalk as it is
on the sidewalk, the world cancels itself.
I see myself losing blows, and pity
the investigator brought to justice, the Carabiniere on the rise.

2

With the levity of one who dreams of being alive
after the chamber clicks shut,
I tear off cellophane, darkness
of an Arabian morning, shimmering.

3

I wake for you, not for the light.
In the mechanical forest the jackrabbits
jump around, turning in its fleshy vortex:
the peacock's enormous point of honor.

Alibi of the Dead Man

Judas says the dead man's alibi
was full of holes: so the dead man went down into the courtyard.
But the alibi was a good one; the dead man was acquitted:
nobody says Judas was wrong.

The coroner says the wounds
are not incompatible with the mechanics of
a fall from above. The newspaper concluded
that therefore the dead man took his own life.

Miserable old people who out of pity
for themselves ought to have died
speak from mirrors, warn us, tell us the future;
they step out of mirrors to kiss the dead.

The assassin was quick to bad-mouth the dead man.
He felt he was an assassin commiserating with a dead man.
He saw himself as an assassin kissing a dead man's forehead.
You see by this that assassins don't overlook the dead.

8:30 P.M. The drunk mourns
8:31 P.M. The gangster reproaches
8:32 P.M. The idiot advises
8:33 P.M. The hangman disposes

The Stock Market's happy, the Stock Market reacts
with splendid, unexpected, soothing vigor
to bulletins from the front, to the proclamations, the certain death
of the Legionnaire killed by the enemy.

Wingless ravens in the flattened
shadows of the balance,
trinity of mercenaries
brandishing the lance.

Judas says: the people cast
stones at my soldiers, so they charged.
No one noticed who was there:
but the Senate concludes Judas isn't wrong.

Don't preach dominance
of one class over another, it's not your job.
Don't say anything that might arouse
class hatred: they're already giving it some thought themselves.

I'm speaking for myself but perhaps even for you.
Friends, let's tell the truth:
we feel happy at feeling oppressed;
it's important to be victims now, and not free afterward.

IV

THE COLDEST
YEAR OF GRACE

The Coldest Year of Grace

The feet that we don't have—
the felt boots that have been stolen from us—
bring us to the snowy marketplace one morning
to sell turtledoves and rabbits,
put together the little cages from stakes
to hide the Siberian cats
in our own fur, half-closed like a wound.

Another life,
our friend with his heavy beard, the shy eyeglasses,
raises with joy
the fish by the tail,
offers it baked to us, or boiled, while
he unwraps it from the newspapers
as if it were night or morning, and nothing raw
were to separate us.

From the numbers, from two numbers, now, you try to understand:
the three albino lion cubs
born yesterday in Australia,
your daughter's albino cat
found dead beneath a tree this morning, in the garden:
those of a short life, they say—this one assassinated.
You give yourself things to do, you multiply, divide
white by white, threat by misfortune.

Once, on the steps, the other time
at a kitchen table
sensing your unthreading life
perhaps (I think of it now) it was

Giorgi and Marzia's death you were trying
to swallow it, spit it out, trying to psychosomaticize it,
robbing it from the future
in two far-off houses . . .

It happened once, it happens to me
in dreams sometimes
from the smoke-covered Franz Joseph
to the great windows of the Südbahnhof
snowed-in city-stretch
impossible coincidence
in the twilight thick with street lamps
before the force of day breaks, forever.

We have friends who take us
to the most famous beer halls,
the waiters going round and round, counting the coasters,
adding up the swans, saints, or lions—
there's no better place in Europe, no warmer, to taste
the gray of midday
from the tiny icy panes
beyond which, invisibly, the defenestration of the apostles goes on.

I love to travel
Oh, how I live to travel
and in the plain, unusual things that can happen
each evening in a different inn
I love to imagine
the small hairy presence
of our household gods
their leaps up against the light, upsy-daisy—
of the cathodic theater.

We leave the house
at an unlikely hour
to study the ground close up
everything's in order or nearly so
it's almost impossible to understand
where so much of an uproar comes from
if in this violet light
the pigeons moan only above, on the cornices.

Never seen so much rain in spring.
Above a thousand meters it's snowing, freezing.
But it's not that, I know.
As soon as you come in dripping, you murmur
we mustn't trust the phone, burn
or throw away the flyers, those little flying things,
in the toilet, the letters, the witches' addresses . . .
My friends, I've already written this poem.

This is the road, I haven't taken
the wrong road this time—wavy, rolling
behind the huge fence. Foreigners
are granted a slow quarantine
between waking and sleeping
between sleep and death before
a limpid eye opens, thinking of
the bicycle and the dogs of Lev Nikolaevič.

Looking at a little box
9 × 21 cm.
with a smooth, sliding cover
I feel young and tired
like my father
he walks around Milan too
three, four months after the heart attack, he planned
on taking some amusement, some distraction.

He or others say you have
to study and while studying, from the top,
try to understand when we betrayed . . .
with whom we betrayed . . . ourselves
and which link held
that wasn't supposed to
and which link we didn't understand
could not have held.

What a funny story; I thought
I was in the middle of the bubble, in the heart,
of the map of the ice
but I wasn't; someone was limping in the vestibule
of the old-new synagogue
someone I couldn't make out
murmuring in a tongue I didn't know
In Milan, the other night, nearly a meter of snow.

The tenderness of the eggshell
softly emptied by your mouth
decorated with far-off landscapes
we're many who think there's no
way to wrap it the way we ought to
so fragile an object, so brief, and so
there's little hope
for the salvation of the eggshell.

V

IN THE DEEP DREAM

Tiny Little Person

When he sleeps he moves only
an ear if you call him.

In dreams he sucks milk
from his dead mama.

He bites biscuits. He loves
coffee grounds.

With his paws he savors
sweaters and shawls.

He sleeps on sheets of paper. He uses
a book for a cushion.

Most of all he's comfortable
in the depths of bureaus, of boxes . . .

Trembling, his eyes going greener
spying on the pigeons coming and going.

He licks his whiskers
for the bug that will fly off.

Sky Blue

Someone, who knows why, with a blanket
on his knees:
in a winter sun, a stingy spring . . .
(It took some time to dig
where I thought you were, the portholes
were black with sand or ice.
Once I got down to you I had
nothing to say, or almost nothing. It was a good thing
not to have found you—even if
you'd never been there.
I'm free and I delight in the earlier
scenario, chaise longues stripped, peeling, overturned
terra-cotta vases and where,
behind the stunted roses, you can guess
the earth's curvature,
the sky blue of Lucca, or Pontedera.)

Serenade

1

She arrives, half magpie and half daughter,
in her clown's jacket, her shirt
three sizes too large,
just barely swaying, modulating
in a sort of flute or whistle
four or five measures of a serenade, a plainchant . . .

2

(The things said between the two of us
during or after the aphasia,
the things said and not said
between you, and the person you are
are probably too few or too many, I wonder
what it's like to travel on after you,
chase after you with a
plane, a liner, a time zone, age?)

3

I give you a hand, I help you
get on your knees, on two paws. I'm afraid
nothing holds you to this dream any longer
of lower corridors, dim, with so many doors,
foggy from the bleach and wardrobes
full of protocol, medicine, straw-filled eagles.
You were supposed to
burst into this scenario—luminous, victorious—and
you don't even appear. You get up
rubbing your eyes,

stretch your young limbs
like a cat in good health
or Gregor Samsa's sister
or as if nothing were important except your
whims, your passions.

The Apartment

1

They say he spends the days
wearing pajamas, a robe. To those
who advise him to go out, to move around, otherwise
his muscles, at his age, will atrophy, his joints
lock up, he responds
with a sweet slow smile.

2

Cavern, bunker, mucous membrane,
dusted books which no one
will read or disarrange,
huge screen measured in millimeters of concentration,
of introjection—and ought
to turn it off, get dressed, risk his skin,
in the muddled air, filled with pollen.

3

He goes wearily, so slowly to the window
to see whether it's still snowing, continuing
in the luminous darkness, there, outside
the infantile disaster of the world.

Hospital Interns

For Bartolo Cattafi

1

. . . the heartbeat
as always when I'm waiting
to leave on a trip—it won't be,
I tell myself, very different from death,
yours for example on the splicing screen
courted, brooded over like an egg,
discussed among friends night after night
as a battle to be lost later, with honor . . .

2

Glare, twilight transparencies
and within, shriveled,
radiant, the sick man, the sick boy trying to dribble past
the goalie of death
helped by the fantastic number of minutes in a day,
of days in a life . . .

3

"Don't leave me alone." And, "If you only knew
how much good it's done me!"
And again, from the half-closed
door, as we walk
contrite through the white space of the corridor:
"Thanks. I'll be expecting you!"
Ah, poor friend, what more will there be
for us to expect? I see
you looking for your glasses, slowly, careful
not to cut off the oxygen line,

to avoid bottles, medicine—and
there now, glasses on your nose searching
in the dusk, adoring
the decrepit body of light,
the last bits and snatches of glimmers from the corners . . .
nothing, nothing more to expect . . .
and yet I know (know
that you're dead, I know it)
you're still a persona, an astute
labyrinth where life
enters and exists, a monument
of little revolving mirrors, a delicate
machine, stupendous . . . How much life
in your having pulled through,
in spite of the odds,
in the gravel, in the thorns of your breath . . .

Madrigal

Down at the bottom . . .
Descended, trembling with pain . . .
But where, come to think of it, I expected
the signs of cocoons, the anguish of albumen,
a full flotilla, happiness
of wardresses of the heat, damp maternal she-dogs
with pointed ears, with a look that's
slow, earthy . . . It's not necessary,
dear souls, to complain
about yourselves, about the mud which, little by little,
you'd dug from the depths . . . Nor laughing
repudiate yourselves in the world
which grows simple, talks nonsense, in the fresh air . . .

Moon

Condition: Seaplane.
But it's not you who flies, no one
flies; home is a moon.
I grope for the foil in the dark, the sponge
to wipe the window dry. I'm on watch,
a cleaner of observatories,
at an altitude of 20,000 millimeters in the starry void,
I spy the abandoned bubble of light, the diving helmet
emptied of its head. I'm a mollusk
gone out a few steps in the direction of death
watching the inside from outside
my conch. Juicy
cell, resinous compartment,
my life's here. It is what it is. From
here, from this projection, I can't change
it, from afar it fulfills me, freezes me.

From the Altar in the Shadows

I strain my ears: is it ever
possible? The sour acid whistle, wrenched
from my dying mother . . . and breath puffs, cracks
of starch, flashes of silver from the altar
of syringes, in the shadows . . . But no,
it's my cat sleeping, it's her cat
breathing, doughy like a grandmother, and I'd
like to give her everything, rummage
in the shadows, overturn
the disguised rosewood altar's
drawers one by one,
oh, all the beautiful pink
coral, the lace collars, the lacquered
boîte with its swallows,
with long gloves cover her hairy claws
if only (memory, memory, how
you make me fail) I could remember the name
of the street, the
number, the floor and where in the house,
in the shadows, in the twilight, the
door, the door, the window, the hole . . .

WESLEYAN POETRY IN TRANSLATION

Translated from the Czech
Mirroring by Vladimír Holan

Translated from the French
The Book of Questions (7 works in 4 volumes) by Edmond Jabès
Le Livre du dialogue by Edmond Jabès
Fables from Old French by Norman Shapiro

Translated from the Italian:
The Coldest Year of Grace by Giovanni Raboni

Translated from the Lithuanian
Chimeras in the Tower by Henrikas Radauskas

Translated from the Portuguese
An Anthology of Twentieth-Century Brazilian Poetry
Brazilian Poetry, 1950–1980

Translated from the Spanish
Off the Map by Gloria Fuertes
Times Alone by Antonio Machado
With Walker in Nicaragua by Ernesto Cardenal

About the Author

Giovanni Raboni was born in 1932 in Milan, where he continues to live and work as an editor for Mondadori Publishers. His first major collection of poems appeared in 1963, and he has remained an important figure in Italian poetry ever since. He is a translator of works in a number of other languages as well, and a critic of contemporary poetry and poetics.

About the Translators

Stuart Friebert is professor of creative writing and directs the writing program at Oberlin College, where he co-edits *Field*, a poetry magazine known for its translation series. He has published ten collections of poems in English and German, and has co-translated Miroslav Holub's *Sagittal Section* and Gunter Eich's *Valuable Nail*, and is the translator of Karl Krolow's *On Account Of: Selected Poems*. He has held a creative writing fellowship from the National Endowment for the Arts.

Vinio Rossi is the McCandless Professor of Romance Languages at Oberlin College, where he teaches French and Italian language and literature. He has published several studies on the works of André Gide, Henri Montherlant, and Paul Claudel, and has co-translated (with Stuart Friebert and David Young) various lyrics of Eugenio Montale and Alfredo Rizzardi.

About the Book

The Coldest Year of Grace was composed in Trump Medieval by G & S Typesetters of Austin, Texas. It was printed on 60 lb. Glatfelter and bound by McNaughton & Gunn Lithographers of Ann Arbor, Michigan. Design by Joyce Kachergis Book Design and Production of Bynum, North Carolina.

Wesleyan University Press, 1985.